Sticky Notes
and Love Poems

Sticky Notes
and Love Poems

I love
You

By Kayla Griffin & Mark Galaviz

First paperback edition February 2024

ISBN 979-8-9875778-5-1
eBook ISBN 979-8-9875778-6-8

Published by Miracle Publishing Group
www.miraclepublishinggroup.com

To us (and anyone in love)—Happy Anniversary.
For lovers and those we love (even our pets).

This book is about all the ways in which we can
love a partner and how we build a life together.

When my husband and I first moved in together, we struggled to find harmony. I am a 100% pure chaotic raccoon and he is retired military. So as you can imagine, he felt overwhelmed by my clutter and I felt disappointed not being able to live up to his standards of cleanliness.

After one of our sillier fights, we sat down and decided we needed to figure this out because we love each other too much to give up. I would like to say I did better at picking things up...but honestly...he just got more open to accepting my mess.

At the time, I was in law school and working two jobs. There were a lot of things that passed me by that should have mattered more...but I was already stretched thin.

I remember telling my husband that I was afraid he would get tired of me and move on with his life. However, he showed me each day that he was planning to stick around.

He would pack my lunch every morning before I left and in it I would find a sticky note. And I would respond with a note hidden around his things. For a full year, he wrote me a note each day...even on the weekends. This book is inspired by the gift he gave me—unconditional and limitless love.

Don't let movies fool you. Love is not a grand gesture. Love is a sticky note repeated each day. It is a poem, a safe space, and constant work.

Love is the decision to appreciate what you have and the willingness to expand who you are to create space for this other person.

This book is to all those who have loved, are in love, and want to fall in love.

It is to my husband—inspired by the nest of sticky notes I have accumulated from him.

Nature

Kayla...

WHEN THE SUN CASCADES

OVER YOU - YOUR FACE
                    YOUR EYES

THE MORNING IS MADE
MORE BEAUTIFUL STILL...
        YOU AMAZE ME MY
        LOVE   MARK

OUR LANGUAGE IS
SPECIAL - WE
HAVE HUNDREDS OF
WAYS TO
SAY
" I LOVE YOU..."

FALL

In therapy I sit in a small circle
Shrinking my body
Forcing myself further away from my past

"Imagine your safe place"
My doctor says
So, I close my eyes and imagine...

The fall

      The orange leaves

The rain

A warm cup of coffee

The

Sound

Of steps

On the pavement

Your smile as we walk back to work

U

YOU ARE THAT
PERFECT SNOWFLAKE
IN MY LIFE- EVERY TIME
I SEE YOU I
KNOW I CAN DO
WONDERFUL THINGS.
I LOVE YOU.

MY BIG "T" TRUTH?
YOU ARE MY SAFE
PLACE, MY REFUGE FROM
THE STORM + MY
HOME - YOU ARE MY
REMEDY FOR ANY AILMENT
AND I AM SO THANKFUL
FOR THEE.

SPRING (by Mark)

She awakens, she snaps and howls with a roar
For Spring now has the whole world to explore
Where the fierce grip of a winter, so sublime
Has had more than enough of its ample time
To coat the world that we all know
To cover the land in ice and snow
Yet, Spring searches deep beneath the earth.
Free from the cold, ready for birth
She finds and plants a seed with power
A mighty tree that one day will tower
This little sprout, grown in a shroud
Soon will make the land so proud
She'll grow tall and fast, straight and true.
She'll touch the clouds, reach the sky so blue
And then the forest will see her tall
The plants and birds will hear her call
This glorious tower, that beacon of light
Will get the land ready for eruption of night
When the land around returns to winter
The time of sunlight, merely a splinter
Spring takes the seed; she holds it close
And while the world is comatose
Spring lays down, holds her little seed
To return to the world in its time of need

FOREST (by Mark)

I
Am
In Awe
The Beauty
The Trees and Sky
The way the Wind blows
It is here, in this place, where
The sacred healing can take place
Time ceases to matter, worries no longer
Hold their power. It is here, in this hallowed space
That I can feel the earth move, and all that remains to us now
Is that we can be in harmony and peace, with everything
that matters
It is only here
That I
Can
Be
Me

OCEAN

You told me once that the ocean takes our sorrow
And every year we try to make it
To the sea

You are so serene and calm when there is salt in the air
And every shell we find
Is a smile

When we find our wishing rock, you close your eyes
And I watch you instead
Praying in silence

You pray and pull your sadness out of your bones
Wrapping the rock your palms
You throw it

The waves take it

I see a healing in you, a renewed purpose
I toss my rock having never
Given a prayer

Little do you know that I watch you when you pray
Because you, my love
Are my ocean

If I
could choose all
over again...

I choose you
Kayla.

I love you so much,
Good luck on your new
project - So proud of you!

Mark.

STARS

When I was a child
I would look out my window

And

Stare intensely at the bright dots
That covered the navy blue night
Praying that a star would fall
So I could make a wish

I felt so small and insignificant
When the stars refused to loosen

But

When I met and married you
I said I've always wanted to wish on a falling star
The one thing I still desperately believed in from childhood
Is that stars that crash have the power
To grant your deepest dreams

And so

You took me to the mountains at 4am
And showered me with meteors
I was overwhelmed by the streaks of light

All my life I thought I was only worthy of one wish
But you gave me more than I could count

I felt so large as if I was the universe
Endless, and full of magic

The irony is - I never made a wish that night
As my deepest dream was already mine

WOLF

The wolf always gets a bad reputation
The Big Bad Wolf
The Wolf in Sheep's Clothing
The Boy Who Cried Wolf

I grew up appreciating their beauty
And strength
But feared their
Sharp teeth and big eyes

In any event, I prefer cats
Their elegance and independence
Their purr notifying me
That I am doing something right

At least, until I met a wolf
With gentle eyes
And a lonely soul
A wolf that didn't bite when I put out my hand

A wolf
My wolf

HOW I FEEL AFTER
YOU TELL ME YOU
LOVE ME IS...
UNSTOPPABLE
POWERFUL HAPPY
+
COMPLETE.
I LOV...

MILLIONS + BILLIONS OF
GALAXIES

COUNTLESS NUMBERS OF
STARS

YET - ONLY ONE
YOU!
¡TE AMO!)

Love,

FOR ME -
THY NAME IS

KAYLA

¡TE ADORO!

RAVEN & WOLF (By Mark)

The rules of the forest are simple:

      If you walk alone, you perish.

            And when the Wolf lost his pack

            The Raven appeared

            And showed him the way

      To Love, to Life

And Together

            The Wolf and the Raven

                made a Home

My RAVEN,

YOU ARE MY STRENGTH +
COURAGE AS I START
MY NEW CAREER, AND
YOU ARE MY GUIDE AND
HEART EVERY DAY.

I LOVE YOU.

I WANT, NEED, +
ADORE THEE ... AND

NOBODY BETTER
MESS WITH STITCH OR
YOU - AND I WILL
CUDDLE THE CRAP
OUT OF THEE MY LOVE!

Waking up next to you is like finding out Santa is real— a lifelong dream made real every morning I love you..!!

You are the intricate part of my mind and soul that gives me life... I love you

NEURONS (by Mark Galaviz)

The human brain contains 100 billion neurons

These neurons form 100 trillion neural connections

    In math, it looks like this: 100,000,000,000,000

That means my mind has more connections with you

Then there are stars in the galaxy

    In my heart, it looks like this: ∞

It's a "Soul Thing"

When my soul
touched yours -
It found love,
It found happiness
It found home.

I love you Katie

...u are the _One_

THE ONE WHO HOLDS MY
HEART,
QUIETS ALL MY FEARS,
AND IS THE ONE PLACE
IN ALL THE WORLD I
CAN CALL HOME... AND,

I love you!

WHENEVER I
DROP YOU OFF I
ALWAYS TELL YOU
HOW LONG UNTIL I
PICK YOU UP...
MY HEART COUNTS
THE MINUTES

AMAZE & INSPIRE ME
LOVE... I KNOW
HARD IT CAN BE TO
THE ROUTINE" BUT YOU
IT AND ARE LOVING
KIND). I THANK YOU SO
MUCH FOR YOU

ROTHKO

Abstract art doesn't make sense
It is a mess and simple at the same time

Anyone can do it
Just scribble

Or paint a dot
Fill in a square

Call it art

It wasn't until I met you
That I understood red

You are my Rothko

YOU ARE MY QUEEN, MY LOVE, AND CHAMPION OF ALL (GRAD) STUDENTS!

PEOPLE WAIT FOR SUN TO SEE IF MORNING - AS FOR ME, WHEN I SEE YOU I KNOW MY DAY CAN TRULY BEGIN

I LOVE YOU!

I USED TO BE AFRAID OF THE DARK, UNTIL I REALIZED YOU ARE MY LIGHT!

I LOVE YOU

My Hopes, my Dreams,
my Path Forward —
You know the way
to all of them
my Heart

I am so
Thankful for
you — Your love
helps me
overcome !

You are my light in
Darkness,
my sun when I am cold —
And my love
every moment.
Thank you for all
you do.

ARTIST (by Mark)

Her brown eyes perceive what others never see

Her song transformed into hope, adrift on the wind

Her trees that hold her vision through time and space

Memories molded into

Her

Dreams given space to

Her life shared with those who have no time nor space

Her art gives us the clarity, lets us dream on the wind

Her canvas floods the mind, allows the soul to be

I
LOVE YOU ONLY
WHEN I
THINK...
BREATH...
WALK...
TALK...
BE... AM...
ALWAYS!

MY HEART
SKIPS A BEAT
WHEN I SEE
YOU.
I LOVE YOU!

GALLERY

Do you remember when
We went to that expensive
Gallery?

The art was so kitsch
But everything was SO
Exorbitant

You couldn't resist the quips
Your sarcastic jaunts at the
Collection

And how you just had to grab
The $30,000 wooden block
Sculpture

My heart dropped into my gut
If it broke we could do nothing but
Run

And for some reason that was
One of those silly moments
That

Made me love you more

Everything

Else

SPREADING

In every empty space I set my things
The counters and tables
My desk...and yours

In every empty space I spread myself
Enveloping everything unclaimed
My studio...your office

Each room filled with me, covering you
My side of the bed...and yours

Anywhere you look you are bound to see me
In the stacks of paper and the books I'll never read
Your shelves...and mine

All my shoes take up the entire closet
My blankets and pillows and snacks
Take up your car

I am spreading...always spreading
As far as I can, every place you have ever touched
Or ever will

I will spread until I fill your entire heart
Your soul, your mouth, your hands
So if I leave this world first
I'll never leave you

GROWING

I am so grateful that you never made me feel
Like we had to have kids to grow
Together

I appreciate how we figured out how to build a family
Full of fur and messes and joy
Together

I love how we are morphing into something
Bigger than just the two of us
Together

The tippy-taps of paws reliant on our care
The chewed sheets from chaos potatoes

The expansion of our love that has
Flowed beyond the rim of our cups

I love what we have become
Together

YOU ARE MY
REASON BEHIND
ALL I DO MY HEART
I LOVE YOU!

YOU ARE MY DREAM
AND WHEN I
AWAKE IN YOUR
ARMS MY HEART
BEATS ANEW.
I LOVE YOU!

HOME (by Mark Galaviz)

```
                My
               Home
There is a place where I feel complete.
This                         place
is                            not
easy            to find       but
one             I   do        seek
for             to  be        whole
That place has always been beside you
```

I WILL ALWAYS CHOOSE
YOU...

THERE IS NO REASON OR
CHOICE FOR ME TO
CHOOSE OTHERWISE—
I WILL ALWAYS CHOOSE
THEE MY LOVE!

8 PM (Love for our dog)

I start to crave a hot cup of decaf
At 8:00 every night

My dog knows the drip of the coffee means
It is time to go out

He waits by the door
Impatiently sighs if I take too long to start the machine

At 8 every night he knows
It is time to play ball
Time to mark his territory
And
Tell the neighborhood dogs, "this is MY home."

I smile every time he sighs at my slowness
A chuckle escapes me when he

Tippy-taps

"Mother, set me free," his eyes say

Sometimes I intentionally go slow
I sprinkle the ground beans a bit at a time
I trickle the water in
And
Scrub the pitcher

He whimpers with annoyance and I laugh

He is old now
And more patient

He no longer sighs as loud

For a moment, I dread the future

The impending crushing sound of silence
At our 8 pm decaf routine

ACHING (to C-3P0, my fur companion)

I wonder why the most beautiful thing
We can be blessed with
Hurts the most
How something so light and lifting
Can change your flesh to
Fragile, cracking, glass
I wonder how something that fills
Your being to the brim
Can leave you an empty shell
Starving for more
How the comfort of companionship
Can leave you so lonely
And aching
Oh, my sweet friend
How joyous your life made me
And how heavy
Your goodbye
Left
Me

You are the

Bestest Part

Of my every

I am. Thank you

for you my Love!

When you breathe

There is always the
air that we shared)
That binds us, no matter

Where we are
and It brings me
back to you.

I love you

We hear about Christmas miracles,
magic, + feelings. The
"Holiday Spirit"... And so much more-
Yet for me you are my
magic, my miracle, + my spirit -
+ I love you.

Quoth my Raven -
"Forevermore"

I love thee.

Every morning you ask me
if you are beautiful.
And I have to lie -
You are not just beautiful-
You are everything!

"Love"

IT JUST MEANS SO
MUCH MORE SINCE
I MET YOU!

¡Te Amo!

I love you
more...

LOVE

Love is the neon sticky note
I found buried in my lunch box

And then a new note the next day

Love is a small moment, not magic
It is a consistent choice to climb

And continue up the mountain

Love is pulling out parts of you
To make more room for more of them

And to fill them up with you

Love is a forever filling cup
You must keep clean and keep pouring

And pouring

Love is a lifestyle
A continuous collaboration

And...

SLEEP

And if you should take the deep sleep
Before me

I will love you still, tomorrow
And tomorrow's tomorrow

And if you should take the deep sleep
Before me

I shall wait with open arms
To love you again

In the next life
And the next...

WHEN I CAN'T SLEEP,
OR AM IN PAIN —
MAYBE FEEL I CANNOT
GO ON..
IT'S YOU THAT HELPS
ME KEEP GOING
I LOVE YOU!

THE MOON, EARTH, +
SUN ALL HAVE THEIR
OWN GRAVITY — YET
YOUR PULL IS THE
STRONGEST ATTRACTION
I HAVE EVER FELT!

I LOVE YOU!

IMMORTAL

I keep trying to make myself permanent

As if these words or these paintings will make me immortal

I want *so* desperately for you to know I was here

Each artwork I make is a bird's song chirping
"I am here, I made it another day."

I want to live eternally
But not in the biblical way

But this way

With this experience

With these eyes

And these words

And this body

Immortal and alive

So, here is another attempt at living forever
Please steal these words and use my tongue

Make me immortal in your heart
Bind me to your soul so that I may never leave

Take me with you in your love

Make me inseparable from the essence of you

Immortal and alive

In your eyes

LOVE RUSHES INTO
MY VEINS,
EMPTYING ME OF
MYSELF & WHAT I
WAS BEFORE
NOW I AM FILLED
WITH THEE -
MY THOUGHTS TURN
TOWARDS YOU ALWAYS
RUMI & MARK

I
BELEIVE IN
THEE KAILA -
I AM ALL-IN
ON US!
I LOVE YOU!

I WOULD
GO TO THE MOON
+ BACK TO BE
WITH THEE!

LOVE, Mark

HAVE YOU
EVER STOPPED
AND WONDERED
WHAT I AM THINKING
ABOUT AT THIS
MOMENT?
IT'S YOU
LOVE
M

WISDOM

Young couples tend to ask their elders
How they made their relationship work

They are desperate for an easy formula
A step-by-step map that will show them the way

Each drop of wisdom they treasure like
The truth of gravity

And yet they are frustrated when the wisdom
Fails to make their relationship work

So, here is my wisdom
Not truth like gravity
But truth like the sun is sure to rise tomorrow
And tomorrow
And tomorrow
Until it doesn't

Relationships only work if you will them to
If you step outside yourself and your own frustrations

They only function if you set aside the formulas
And experiment, and play, and follow your curiosity

They only last if you, ever so annoyed and hurt
Choose *them* over the pain, because the alternative is
worse

Choose them

SICK

I am in a lucid, hazy dream
My body aches
My soul tires

I feel a warm blanket drawn
Up over my shoulders
A small comfort

Warm lips press against my forehead
My dream pauses
As I realize

You have come to nourish me
To soothe the aches
To calm the fever

To heal me

WHEREVER YOU ARE,
MY HEART IS WITH
THEE.

〇DAY, JUST BREATHE
KNOW YOU ARE
WONDERFUL MY LOVE

love you
—
3 WORDS THAT
CONTAIN MY WORLD

THANK YOU FOR YOU BASI

TIE ADORO!

KAYLA
ANY
LIST I
MAKE,
ACCOMPLISH-
MENT,
OR GOAL
IS ALL
BECAUSE OF
YOU!

I LOVE
YOU!
MARK

IT'S AMAZING THAT YOU ARE THE KIND OF PERSON THAT ONCE ONE ~~DOES~~ SPENDS TIME WITH YOU, ALL I WANT TO DO IS SPEND MORE — YOU ARE MY HAPPY PLACE! LOVE, MARK.

REASON #53
THE WAY YOUR EYES COMMAND A ROOM, SEEK OUT INFORMATION, & MORE MY HEART JUMPS! I LOVE YOU.

WOTD — LONGING
WHENEVER WE SEPARATE — FOR WORK, SCHOOL, ETC — I LONG TO RETURN TO YOUR ARMS, EYES & SOUL. I LOVE/LIVE YOU.

WARMTH

Please wrap me up tightly

In a warm blanket

Fill my cup with hot tea, or cocoa, or coffee

Put fuzzy socks on my feet

And lay me next to a heater

For I cannot replace the warmth

Of being tightly wrapped in your arms

Your touch heating my stomach

Your warm skin thawing my icy feet

Your body, my heat

It is impossible to crawl out of bed

To separate myself from you

And go to work

BLUE

Blue car when we first met
Blue eyes

Bluebird of happiness
Ocean blue

Van Gogh's Starry Night
The TARDIS

The moon in our tattoos
Your favorite color

My reminder I am loved

EVERYTHING

Everything about love has been said before
There is no unique way to express
That you mean...

...Everything to me

I am at a loss on how to tell you
That I cannot imagine
A life without you

There are no more creative ways
To paint
Or sculpt
Or capture

Exactly what you mean to me

So I will stick with the best ones

I love you
I need you
I want you

I LOVE YOU MORE
THAN TACOS... OR

TUESDAY —
OR TACO TUESDAY!
(OR ANYTHING ELSE, BUT
I WANTED TO BE
SPECIFIC!) ☺ !!
TE AMO.

BETWEEN HEART,
MIND, + SOUL —
YOU'VE CAPTURED
ME — AND I
WANT TO FOREVER
STAY WITH THEE

SOME PEOPLE ARISE IN THE
MORNING AND AWAKE FROM THEIR
DREAMS...
BUT IN MY CASE, YOU ALLOW THE
DREAM TO CONTINUE EVERY DAY MY LOVE.
— TE ADORO KAYLA

AS THE MOON BEAMS,
AND THE SUN SHINES -
MY LOVE IS AGLOW
FOR THEE ALWAYS

I HAVE NEVER
WANTED TO RUN AWAY
WITH SOMEONE SO BADLY
AND THAT'S THE CATCH
I FALL FOR YOU BECAUSE
YOU MAKE US STAY +
FIGHT.   I LOVE
                  YOU.

SEE? EVEN THE
PICTURE + SAYING
PROVES WE LOVE
EACH OTHER -
IN EACH OTHERS
SUBCONSIOUS WE KNOW
WHAT THE OTHER FEELS
#REALLOVE   #LOVEREAL
#HASHTAG#   #HUH?

WORDS (by Mark Galaviz)

Words/phrases that detail our love:
Potatoes
"Why did you do that?!"   "Hi, I'm Kayla"
You, sitting at my computer...again...after I lost a
password
Baby Wipes
Korean Dramas and Kisses
A look in your eyes when you just KNOW what the other
is thinking
The Nook
That moment at the coffee shop and later at the
construction site
"You like that you fucking idiot?"
Shooting Stars
$1.25
Road trips and the best game ever invented
Chocolate
That orange article of clothing left in some hotel room
Not Wash
Reno, Nevada
Little tokens given to each other at the tree farm
Shopping
Late night cheap Totino's Pizza
A bedroll and soup
Camping
Farming games...15,000,000 effing farming games
Raccoons
3:00 am drives from the middle of nowhere
Forever

EVERY NOTE (by Mark Galaviz)

Every Note
        That I have ever sent
Is about a moment

How you made me feel
                        Happy,
                Loved,
            Wanted,
        Needed,

    Every Note
That I ever send
        Makes that moment

            Last Forever

HOW I FEEL AFTER... TELL ME YOU...

I WILL ALWAYS CHOOSE... YOU

MY FAVORITE PART OF
MY VACATION (OR DAY)
IS SIMPLY TO LOOK
OVER, SEE YOUR EYES
AND FEEL LIKE HOME

I LOVE YOU!

LIKE THE
UNIVERSE...
SO DOES MY
LOVE FOR...
EVERY D...
TE AMO!

D: CLOSE
WE GROW
IMAGINE...
E TWO
...
EVE...
ACH...

INTO ME...
HOLD ME OU...

BOOK

I wrote these poems
In this book

Because it will outlast us

Someday we'll be found
In the dust

Of an old bookstore

And if one person chooses
To read this

After our bodies

Have crumbled to ash
And we've left

Then they will know

Just how much we have loved
How much two

Strangers have loved

WILL ALWAYS

AT YOUR TIRAMISU

MY HEART! ☺

I LOVERS THEE

YOU ALWAYS
BE MUH
JUICY GEL!
MUAH!!
(I LOVE YOU,
SORRY I'M A
DORK!)

KAYLA,

DON'T FORGET...

I LOVE YOU, AND

TOGETHER WE SHALL GO
AND DO WONDROUS THINGS!

♡ MARK

You —
ARE SO DAMN SMART —
& THIS THESIS —
WILL BE SLAUGHTERED!

I FRIGGIN,
LOVE YOU.

Love

WE ARE BOTH TEACHERS
+ STUDENTS -
AND TOGETHER LETS
HAVE A CLASS THAT
LASTS FOREVER

KAYLA,
WHEN YOU
AWOKE THIS
MORNING —
MY HEART BECAME
ALIVE

I LOVE YOU!

About the Authors

Once upon a time, Kayla & Mark fell in love, the same way most people do. Unexpectedly and terrified

Full of every cliche:

friendship
    then love
and then came a family full of fur.
Today they still make promises
and write notes

They choose each other
over
and over
and over again
And they are living happily ever after...

www.ingramcontent.com/pod-product-compliance
Lightning Source LLC
Chambersburg PA
CBHW051552120626
46551CB00013B/1476